The Hand of the Midnight Moon

Selected Poems

John Forrest Harrell

The Hand of the Midnight Moon

Selected Poems

Copyright © 2017
by
John Forrest Harrell

All rights reserved.

This work, or parts thereof, may not be reproduced in any form, written, electronic, recording, or photocopy, for internal use or sale without written permission from the copyright holder.

Published in the United States of America by

Brendan Printing House
18543 Yorba Linda Boulevard
Yorba Linda, California 92886

BrendanPrintingHouse@gmail.com

ISBN 978-1-946347-00-8

Forward

Greetings and salutations from the environs of my home in Yorba Linda, California, where gracious living (as it says on the license plate holders) is the rule—unless the !@#&% *Santanas* (an Indian word meaning *Devil Winds*) blow! The television meteorologists claim the winds picked up the name *Santa Anas* in the 1920s because they blew through the Santa Ana Canyon from the northeast and on into Orange County. My grandmother, who grew up on her grandfather's ranch in the southern San Joaquin Valley near Bakersfield, insisted there was no Santa Ana Canyon there in the 1890s when she was a girl and the name was *Santanas*. I stand with Grandma on this!

I've finally completed a serious attempt to make good on a promise I made to the late Jerry Palley, among others who are still alive, that I would assemble some of my poems into a book for publication. He had been a Spanish Literature professor and was the Editorial Chair of the *California Quarterly (CQ)*, the journal of the California State Poetry Society (CSPS). I am grateful to Jerry for sifting through my collection of poems more than two decades ago, as well as for his encouragement, his sense of whimsy and his appreciation for how I used the language.

I also want to thank several other CSPS folks for helping me. I thank Kate Ozbirn, another fine poet, a former Literature professor, former President of the CSPS and Editorial Chair of the *CQ*, for her attempts to get me to civilize some of the verses. I thank Margaret Saine, a multi-lingual poet, a former Spanish Literature professor, a member of the Executive Board of the CSPS, and a *CQ* Editor, for her careful review and comments on the draft.

I wrote the poems in this little volume off and on—to be fair, mostly off—over the past fifty years, many of them twenty years ago when I was active in *The Valley Poets*. It was and is a remarkably productive working poetry group in Glendora, California, founded and still run by CSPS Vice President/Communications and former *CQ* Editor Keith Van Vliet. Keith's sense of humor and keen observations shine forth in his poetry, of course, but his encouragement and his example were a major inspiration for me during the 1980s and 1990s when I was active in the group. He, too, has reviewed and commented on the draft, for which I am grateful.

I've included a few earlier pieces in the collection that have a little different perspective than that of the bulk of the work. I propose they are indicative to some extent of my journey—of my evolving awareness of the finger of God at work (and play) in me and in the world around me. A number of the poems have appeared in the pages of the *CQ* over the decades, but otherwise they have been read here and there and have not been published heretofore.

This has been more than a little work for me. Over fifty years, even poems produced in dribbles and drabs wind up being a lot to review and from which to cull a selection for publication.

My colleagues on the Executive Board of the CSPS and on the *CQ* Editorial Board can be blamed for encouraging me but *not*, however, for whatever hubris or insanity appears in the pages that follow.

I hope you enjoy the poems. Generally, the little beggars have been hanging around for a long time.

John Forrest Harrell
Yorba Linda, California
January, 2017

Table of Contents

Gentle Caress 11
White Mountain 12
Anno Domini MCMLXXXIX 13
Santa Claus 13
Curves and Lines 14
The Water Gate 15
Easy Does It 15
Between Sinner and Saint 16
My Grandfather's People 17
Old Times, End Times, New Times 18
Hurless Barton Park 20
Marriage 21
Fog's Night Mysteries 21
How Precious Her Happiness 22
Wanderlust 23
Not Free Enough to Try 23
Between Weed and Grain 24
Living Through It All 25
The High Road 26
Yorba Linda Sabbath 26
In the Dalliance before the Dawn 27
Every Day in Every Way 28
The Eyes of God 29
Interlude 30
South of Mendocino 31
Just for the Record 31
The Fountain of Youth 32
The Melody that Never Was 33
The Butterfly 34
I Pray You, Comrade Chairman, Go Gently 35
It Is Good 36
On Tour 37
The American Dream 38
With Apologies to Paul 39
For Bud 40

Post-Traumatic Grief Grace 41
After the Summer Fires 42
Down in Hollywood 43
The Devil Winds 44
The Monsoon Season 45
Bright Daggers of Light 46
Sunrise on the Santa Fe Trail 47
Miss Andrea 48
The Florida Keys 49
When the World Came Down 50
Crusader Rabbit 51
The Capstone 52
Never Mind, Gautama 52
Castles in the Sand 53
High Mass 54
The Mud Pie Party (A Painting) 54
Merlin's Passing 55
Yorba Linda Celebration 56
Buddha on the Mountain 57
The View from Murchison Park 58
White Lace at Low Tide 59
Cigarette Spirits 60
Hope 61
Morning's Eyes 62
Navajo Respite 63
Apology for Winter 64
Sierra Valley Shower 65
Power 66
Perspective 66
The Tucson Table 67
A Still, Small Wind 68
The Three Musketeers 69
Valedictory for Megan 70
The Leader 71
The Mountain Corral 72
Solitary Moon Night Sky 73
Laguna in the Winter 74

Evensong for Helena ... 75
San Francisco's Intermission ... 76
Day's End ... 76
Mesa Verde ... 77
Mister Matt ... 78
Grand Canyon Treasure ... 79
Winging West ... 80
Deus ex Machina ... 80
The Whistling Wind and the Crashing Sea ... 81
Noble ... 82
Semi-Precious and Incomplete ... 83
Perspiring Perspective ... 84
Circles Within Circles ... 84
Always Aloft ... 85
The Fruit of the Tree ... 85
Peace in Our Time ... 86
Karmic Strings ... 86
The Mystery of the Pipes ... 87
Autumn Leaves ... 88
Canary ... 88
Sparkles of Golden Sunshine ... 89

For Madame Pamela

Gentle Caress

The hand of the midnight moon paints quiet shadows
                            around the cares
               and concerns
        of the city's busy denizens,
    boxed as we are into squares
             of noisy sameness day by day.
For a few nights every month the beacon light tugs softly
     at our hearts and souls
                   and pulls them with its mystery
        into the infinite variety
            and elegant calm
                of eternity.
In the respite, if at all, there is remembrance
                       and new resolve.
But human memories fail after repeated muggings,
     and what is out of sight
          drifts in time
                  beyond the mind as well.
So every month the beacon light returns
               to leave us reminders.
And the hand of the midnight moon paints quiet shadows.

White Mountain

The old stone rises high over the countryside
And in the setting sun blazes and burns
Many colors into the eyes of the settlers.
Down in the mountain where it is crushed
And stripped of its golden veins,
The rock is pure white and seems
A clean tablet that has no experience;
But where it rises upthrusting from the ground
It is changed magnificently.
Few even guess the grand old peak is the same stone.
Where the elements have beat at it and lashed it,
And caressed it and warmed it,
The lines are deep and full of character.
Its spaces rise with the textures of life
And with the knowledge of many kingdoms.
The ancient rock is stained in swirling shapes,
Organic patterns moving in dimensions of centuries.
Where there is any white in this part of the stone
There is sharp contrast all around;
It is colored here by experience

> *And not by innocence.*

Anno Domini MCMLXXXIX

The year's great gifts have all been levied out,
And nothing very much remains with which to play
The grandiose games of Tolstoy's tortured work.

Involved so long in conflicts all around the world,
The pawns have simply, respectfully but firmly,
Declined their worn-out seats and turned to knights.

They stand now shivering in the wintry streets
And proclaim their liberty with brittle happiness.

In the New Year nation shall rise with nation
To put the building's blocks and mortar into place
And then each soul will step forthrightly out
To vote with all its fellows whether they'll be

> *Freemen or slaves.*

So begins the time of answering:
Is there any slavery more honest or more hopeless than
Slavery chosen by the serfs for their security?

Santa Claus

Hello! Please come in!
Hi. I'm from the government.
I'm here to help you!

Curves and Lines

The butterflies flutter gently in the air,
Drawn to what pleases them,
Their dalliance full of light and color;
And the fixed purpose of straight lines
Bends slowly by fascinated impulses
Into arcs that tarry, twist and turn,
Breathing deeply the perfume
Of what attracts their hearts,
Then unraveling in aimless meanderings.

The heart is older, wiser than the mind,
And knows the time is still a little off
For weapons, canons and consistency
To change our lives and conform our world.
The rumblings are only rumors yet
And with focus still can be ignored.
And there is this in the Music of the Spheres:
Fixed or fluttering,
Which is purpose, and which is play?

The Water Gate

Though it's a small and strangely-shaped gate,
The one at the well-side of the town
Spills slender glimpses of its treasures
Into the parched barrenness around.

Even those with slim, quiet camels,
Moving through the night and slipping by,
Cannot enter through the passageway,
Cannot sneak to thread the needle's eye.

Yet humble men with ought on their backs
But what honesty and toil have spawned,
Move through the oddly-shaped gate with ease;
And, rested up, leave again at dawn.

Easy Does It

The great irony of life is,
By the time a man learns
To follow wisdom's urgings,
So that he no longer creates
Harm or trouble for himself,
So that life flows happily,
Like a smooth dance or a good song,
So that his graceful smile
Is so overwhelming it warms our lives
And we are left to wonder, to remark
How easy things are for him,
The great irony of life is,
His life is almost over.

Between Sinner and Saint

The fading arrow of ancient, crumbling asphalt
Begins at the horizon's hills, runs straight
Through playgrounds of cactus and chaparral
To bare soles of feet planted quietly alone.
In the far-off light the road is mesmerizing,
Simple, clear and full of fascinating dreams.
Only there, where there is no experience,
No memories to clutter guiding precedent,
To twist and cloud what's right and wrong,
Only there, where theory and conjecture reign
To choose the flags of friends and foes,
Only there, in the far distance, is the line
Sharp and distinct, crisp and still in focus,
Between honed purpose and overruled wilderness.

What begins as a clean and sterile slice
Through so many useless nuisances of worlds
Is always tempered with ages of experience.
The old highway is mixed in many places
With the uncivilized audacity of the desert.
Up close, the edges of the road are worn,
With whole chunks missing, filled with sand.
There is even now life in the fast lane—
The dozing lizards, scorpions and snakes.
Nearby, in the pleasant sunshine, it is spring
And the fine edge is blurred and unimportant
Next to the plants, which lift their colors,
And the birds, which skitter, bob and cheep,
Celebrating in and around and through it all.

My Grandfather's People

My grandfather's people
Had lived so many generations
In the hills and valleys of eastern Tennessee
That nothing with them
Had ever come from another place.
Even the dancing, it was said, came from there.
No one spoke of the time
When the wagons came over barely rutted roads.
No one spoke of the time
When the fields were forests.
And no one spoke of the time
When men of another color received them kindly.

But in the sameness of closed-in horizons
And completely unquestioned expectations,
My grandfather grew itchy, it was said.
The look in his eyes confused his neighbors
And made his cousins uncomfortable.
Finally, early one spring morning
At the beginning of the century,
He stepped away, stepped west,
And made his own connection with his roots.

Old Times, End Times, New Times

The town is quiet, tense with stiff smiles.
Questions and cares swirl among, around,
Run silently behind the stares and shrugs.
How will Skowhegan survive with no bedrock?

The mill abides, rising now
In tiers above the worn cobblestones,
Beside the dam that first tamed
The river twenty decades back.
There are no cars around it now,
No groups of workers waiting.
The bare, swinging light bulbs
Usually shining into the night
Through the dirty, arched windows
And the open doors are dark.
The noises made by the mill,
The rumbles and clacks, are gone.
The massive black machines
On the ground floor are catatonic.

The young lady on the Kennebec Bridge
Stares up at the night sky,
Seeing nothing and lost
In the accusations of her own remorse.
She hears only failure—
After seven generations, failure.
Off and on, she exhales,
Her warm breath condensing in a pillar
Like a noiseless steam whistle
Signifying the silent arrival
Of the end of the shift,
Or the chapter, or maybe the book.

The ornate old key she clutches
Came from the entry of the mill,
From the massive oak door,
Where it had been a symbol of stability.
Now it is merely old brass,
Burning its burden into her heart.
As the night wears on, she wonders,
Again and again with meaningless differences:
Would her father or her grandfather before her
Have done anything she did not?

Finally, in the dark silence before
The dawn stretches colored fingers
Across the benighted landscape,
Her heart hears nothing—
No ringing confirmation, no words of comfort,
But no clamoring accusation, either.
The thing is done and over,
The world has turned as it always does.
Her wounds have not healed, but so what?
She sighs and finally accepts
The simple truth of the coming, rising sun.

Slowly and with tears hung upon her lashes,
The young lady who is the last of the line
Tosses the key off the silent stone bridge,
On into the covering waters of the Kennebec.

Hurless Barton Park

The people gather in the late afternoons on Sundays
When the shadows of the trees are stretched over the grass
By gentle breezes offered up to the evening from the sea.
It is a time when the heat of high summer has mellowed
And the weekend's finish is just around the corner.
Picnic dinners and lawn chairs are spread on blankets
For mothers and fathers, grandparents and aunts.
As the music begins the little ones ride bicycles around
And along the cement paths, only once in a while falling off.
Between the playing there is applause and also smiles.
The park and the concerts seem always to have been there,
And we who listen and enjoy are merely taking our turns
In a dance that lasts hundreds of years and beyond,
Swirling through changing fashions and different music,
Always in the same pleasant respite just before nightfall,
Just before the business of the next week starts.
But Hurless Barton Park was created two years ago
Out of an old field that had long since lost its crop.
The trees that seem forever rooted here
Were brought in on large trucks and lifted into big holes
By giant, noisy cranes, smelling of diesel and operated
By swearing, sweating men in undershirts and hard hats.
The hills and gentle slopes were pushed rudely into place
By other loud machines, both harsh and uncompromising.
As the music dances through the trees again, my head clears
And these little confusions of fact blur the scene no more.
Since long centuries of tradition begin somewhere or when,
What really was is of little consequence in the places we live
And only dreams anchor us in the river of time.

> *Held steady there by our common myths*
> *And shared expectations,*
> *Murmuring my own amen,*
> *I lift my hopes and splash in midstream.*

Marriage

The calls of little creatures by the lake
Were gentle music floating on the breeze.
The day had quieted down with the dusk;
It was a perfect time to take our ease.

We shaped our hearts in silence even then
And there the base of marriage was begun,
A warmth; then many memories of our love—
The sacrament, our choosing both and One.

Fog's Night Mysteries

In the dark and damping nights the fog rolls in
And what before was simply spreading eventide
Now becomes the entryway to dreams and mysteries.
There is no middle ground of open comfort here.
There is only moving out into the misting world,
Clamping caps and girding jackets tight about
And moving bravely through the open, foggy spaces
To a grand and almost endless, larger destiny;
Or there's curling close with other siblings
Bunched together in a den about the cozy fire,
Giggling with the warming comfort of the clan
Against the threats of ghostly mysteries beyond,
With parents going one to one, holding, laughing;
After tucking sleepy children tightly into bed.

How Precious Her Happiness

Waking in the morning
With the sunlight streaming across our bed,
Lighting up the blond swirls of her hair
And dancing in her lashes,
I wonder at how quietly she sleeps.
When she moves finally and turns,
Feeling me next to her
And smiling in her dreams,
I remember that she loves me.
Not really understanding, almost confused,
It pleases me anyway,
As if I've stumbled on a part of my purpose.
Moving on with a smile of my own,
Holding, cuddling her in her sleep,
I remember again
How precious her happiness is to me.

Wanderlust

The weeds wander over the old hard soil,
Crass entrepreneurs out for the fast life
And growing anywhere there is sustenance.
They break open the ground and prepare it,
Giving rise first to dreams and then to
Gardens built with the might of monopoly.
Although some remain, trimmed and shaped,
Most move on out into unattended lands,
Abandoned and old or uncharted and new,
And once more wander, without any rules.

Not Free Enough to Try

Whither the breeze blows
Is a wonderful land
Full of white temples
And soul-stirring music,
Flowing over with peace
And laughter and wisdom,
Never failing our needs
And always fulfilling.
It is a land denied us,
Not because it isn't ours,
Not because we cannot go
If we wish, but simply
Because we won't follow
Whither the breeze blows.

Between Weed and Grain

See, the Master taught us long ago
To raise the weeds with the grain.
He told us to collect them at the end
And burn them in their own place.

See, but growing old I've learned
He didn't quite tell the whole truth.
The weeds are different, mind you,
And not really the same as the grain.

See, what my blurred old eyes say to me is,
They are valuable in *ungrainly* ways
And maybe worth more than a bonfire.
What I swear is true these days is that

See, when the Master told us to put off
Our judgment between weed and grain,
He wasn't saving the weeds.

Living Through It All

Let me sing to you a living song, the song of life itself,
And take you with me down the canyons of experience
And dance the waltzes, jitterbugs and foxtrots on and off.
And let me share with you the far-off dreams and whims
No certified and sane one even speaks about today.
And let me hold you close when we begin to cry
For expectations left awash and empty, never filled,
And tragedies that leave our souls bereft of God.
And let me pray with you to keep our courage strong
When fears and fright take over more than what we will.

With the changing times that spring upon us unaware,
And what we do to play and change and play again,
It is our sharing in the miracle that yields the blessings,
And the living through it all that is the endless mystery.

The High Road

Patterns of crushed raindrops
And swirling mists
Are visiting our careful world
Of structure and cement.
Quiet flees with silver flashes,
Bridging billowing pillows,
Then hides from celestial symphonies
Spilling grandly and grumbling back.
On the walk beside my door
A centipede bends almost in half,
Found out and frightened in the flash.
I in my temple take another road;
I have a mind of another bent
And burn incense.

Yorba Linda Sabbath

Early on each Sunday morning,
Up by the old, worn reservoir,
Only the birds make sounds,
Make frames for an easy peace.
The homes that border on
The oak-shaded lane are still.
In the reflection imposed
By the soft and careful quiet,
The struggles of the week past
And the ambitions for the next
Slip away from center stage
And God speaks softly, gently,
Between the avian bells.

In the Dalliance before the Dawn

There is peace in the dalliance before the dawn.
The quiet keeps the heart at rest
And turns the mind to gentle thoughts
Of how the puzzles all go back to God.
And then the birds begin to stir.

The isolated cheeps of different kinds start slowly,
Waking others who join with the trickle of sounds,
And still others, adding, forming streams,
Adding, swelling into rivers,
And still adding, running together in a torrent.
Finally, the cacophonous symphony of thanksgiving
Pours over the bulwarks of silence,
Everywhere inundating with individual *amens*
From hundreds of tiny beaks
And tiny, praising little spirits.

As shadows come out of the night,
Passing through gray outlines and into familiarity,
The dawn arrives and the chorus recedes.
Over the rest of the day, the little spirits
Eat and preen and feed their families,
And fly with the patterns of their kinds.
They put forth their prayers of praise
In busy making-do with gifts and responsibilities
Of industry, commitment and accomplishment;

But as the sun sets and they settle in their nests
For the intermission of the night,
They dream richly, with security and with joy,
In anticipation of the praise-filled chorus they will join
In the dalliance before the dawn.

Every Day in Every Way

I am there
>	For the proud
>>		Who are sure of salvation.

I am there
>	For the purgers
>>		Who clean cellars of men.

I am there
>	For the wobbling winos
>>		Who stumble on the steps.

I am there
>	For the lovers
>>		Who feel sinful in their bliss.

I am there
>	For the children
>>		Who blink and break rules.

I am there
>	For the humble
>>		Who sit quietly in corners.

And I am even there
>	For every sermon
>>		Every seventh day.

How do I dare?
>	Go figure.
>>		If you dare.

The Eyes of God

See, they said, how powerful are the eyes of God,
How unstoppable the fury of his wind and sea.
I looked for his love and didn't see him there.

See, they said, how grand are the eyes of God,
How magnificent the peaks and valleys of his land.
I looked for his love and didn't see him there.

See, they said, how fine are the eyes of God,
And lifted high a jeweled chalice glinting light.
I looked for his love and didn't see him there.

See, they said, how just are the eyes of God,
How unrelenting his inspection of our lives.
I looked for his love and didn't see him there.

See, they said, how pretty are the eyes of God,
And twirled their creations of sticks and yarn.
I looked for his love and didn't see him there.

As I cried in my failure and frustration,
I felt a paw on my knee and looked up into
The dark brown, limitless eyes of my dog.

Interlude

Winging east, the pancake layers of clouds
Create their own worlds
And I fly with them above and below me,
A wide and flat land of magic.
The snow flurries of Chicago are behind me,
The headaches of New York and New Jersey wait for me
Still miles beyond the limits of my sight.

Soft and mellow fluff ball hills and valleys of white cloud
Stretch out forever underneath
And I know I can bounce and slide and run all day up here
And never face the storms below.

In the middle of my glee, the airplane moves from under
Flat layers of stretched white cotton
And into the bright sunlight.
There is a round rainbow on the clouds below
With a flat black airplane shadow in its center.
       I am, after all, not playing up here by myself.
           I am, after all, only in transit.
               I am, after all, tied to the earth
And to the struggles that bluster across her face.

Ah, but for now, this is my rest and my playground.
I make no conclusions and pursue no points.
In the lovely sunlight, across the soft, white landscape,
I lift my cup of gentleness and joy.
Whatever remains for me in the craggy spaces down below,
I am *wrapt* in this quiet kingdom of peace,
Where the pancake layers of clouds create their own worlds.

South of Mendocino

The land, untamed and wild,
    Awoke with its craggy face to the stars;
        Yawning, groggy still, it smiled.

And the oats, whiskery seas,
    Murmured in a random diligence,
        Busied by the night breeze.

And the wind whispered lies,
    And all manner of things, ghostly and pale,
        Beneath the chill of the skies.

Frothing in the thrill of mystery,
    The shadows bowed and strutted by the moon,
        Flitting, solid, real, then silvery.

Just for the Record

I winnow the purposes of men's minds
Into gray shades of reality and myth.
I see love in the hurtfulness of men
And wait for it because I know it outlasts
The wounds and scabs of outrage and fear;
Although some survive with hatred,
There is no healing without love
And there is no future without it.

The Fountain of Youth

Her emotions huff, rise and fall
Over lines of love and hate, her eyes fill with cold fury
For multitudes, for possible failures of plutonium fires,
And for animals maybe mistreated by insensitive handlers.
She flashes brightly and then fades to sneers for old lovers
Who misunderstood their roles and failed her expectations.
She is pretty, slender, and moves boldly with sure gestures,
But they are punctuated somehow
      with moments of uncertainty,
So that I want to touch her,
      to protect her,
           to support her.

Even as I think such thoughts,
      I am much too shy to move.
I cannot give the reassurance I conjure as a gift for her.
She would misspell my honest concern
      as sneaking sexuality.
Surely, she would; so I listen to the language of her poems
And offer my own quiet praise
      for her growing, glowing gift.
I love her strong commitments,
      but I don't truck with them.
In my middle age and particular experience
      I have no energy
For millions beyond my ken,
      nor for animals I've never seen.
And I prefer to put the heat of my heart into the tragedies
I have hope in some small way of changing for the better.

There is another aspect to our different times of life.
Watching her reject old lovers with a cold, righteous scorn,
I think of my first wife, not of the betrayal and the pain,
But of the sweet hot love I held in my young heart for her
And how it lingers in me still.

The Melody that Never Was

It is a mood, an eclipse by the moon.
The vintage music is a fleeting song.
Here only moments, and left me too soon.

The memory jars like a spilled spittoon,
Pulls at the middle of the cocktail throng.
It is a mood, an eclipse by the moon.

The knotted visage is a tell-tale rune
Of love failing dreams and going off wrong.
Here only moments, and left me too soon.

The eyes turn inward at the special tune,
A sweet, soft sound, but still a bitter song.
It is a mood, an eclipse by the moon.

The knife cools down, the sigh is not a swoon,
The pause retires, the chatter moves along.
Here only moments, and left me too soon.

Surely, mixing tribes was the road to ruin.
We were unwise then and silly, headstrong.
It is a mood, an eclipse by the moon.
Here only moments, and left me too soon.

The Butterfly

Days of gray, and grayer nights,
These first few hours beyond the jail
Have made me think of me.
Of blacks and whites my character
Was molded mushy-firm,
Though through it all played still the gray
Of holy, peaceful Gothic vaults.
Hard and fast, my mind made up,
So did I seize the right to scorn
What didn't fit my manufactured norms.
I agreed to the games and cheered them on.
Lost in logic lies and punched computer cards,
I only yearned for liberty.

Now, I stumble forth in the brightest light,
A changed and chary son
Of childhood blinking innocence.
I know the rules and hear dividing words.
I see around me all the marching martinets,
But the bad guys and the good guys
Have all blurred in sunny shades of sympathy.
When I see the white knights
Coming to rescue the lady in distress
I know the difference lies
In where my shadow falls.

I am alive to move and choose and love.

I will seek the breadth and depth
And peace of me
To make my home infinity.

I Pray You, Comrade Chairman, Go Gently

Will you go down the sacred halls of history
Slinking along dark sides?
The swelling voices sing now for liberty,
Spilling songs over ramparts,
But they can be tempered and turned to dirges
With your fearsome fists.

Is there any reason for the chains
You impose on your own kith and kin,
Or is it just a sickness leaking
From the devastated pith of your soul?

Will you take your place as
One of the guiding fathers, giving vision,
Bringing the multitudes home to
The glory of their bright horizons now?

Or will you fight against the tides
And fling your spittle in the wind?

Will your own countrymen, your neighbors once,
Revile you and despise you,
And quietly teach their children and grandchildren
To call you monster?

Oh, antiquated, anachronistic Caesar!
Let the lovely children be free!

I pray you, go gently down the halls of history;
Walk the center spaces where there is light
And feel instead their blessings,
The generations thanking God for you.

It Is Good

I say to you, cockroach,
That light and dark are relative,
That yin and yang
Ebb and flow, separate and mix,
That principles wander over the landscape.

I say to you, cockroach,
Their consequences flit and flutter stupidly.
I say these things and you repeat them,
But do not miss the life
I choose to live behind my words.

I say to you, cockroach,
Although good and evil
May have no meaning beyond eternity,
Their cause-and-effect
Is the reason for this world.

And I say to you, cockroach,
Pick whatever principles you want,
Whatever fits you well,
And believe deeply, passionately, so that
It becomes you, what fits you well.

On Tour

In the unfamiliar countryside
Of strange and foreign lands,
Without parents and wife and children
To touch me and to comfort me,
The clouds drift by a full moon
In the quiet of the night,
Silver shrouds draping themselves on airy couches
In front of the globe lamp
That breaks the deep dark of eternity.
In the sudden yearning of my heart
I am comfortable again,
Not because I am home,
But because I am equally far from home.

The American Dream

The yellow flame flickers lightly in my Uncle's tomb
And dances with the sounds of crickets in the night.
In the shadows it throws on the walls of the rotunda
I see the shades of his friends and fellow soldiers.
They were strong, mighty warriors in their own time,
But here they walk only as adjuncts and lieutenants,
Assisting in the power and the presence of my Uncle.
Now, when the lamp lifted by his Lady has not light,
When her lovely, flowing robes are sullied and torn,
When every battle of the war is lost to politicians,
I come into the calming quiet and remember eternity.
In this place the vision of my Uncle is overwhelming
And the certainty and direction of his loving dreams
Are set in nature, to be the future for all mankind.

The shadows move the yellow flame with their whispers:
Let us be free, let us be free, Lord, let us be free.

With Apologies to Paul

Love redeems the world
        and has not lost her saving sight.
She eyes the clanking gongs
        and she knows she makes them right.
She sees the world of heroes
        in shades of mottled gray.
Though triumphs make her smile,
        she knows their feet are clay.
She endures all things;
        she is patient and always kind.
She believes what is good,
        but not because she's blind.
Oh, no, love's not sightless here
        nor ever was she that—
Although her kid sister,
        romance, is blind as a bat!

For Bud

Corporal Henry B. Ginther
United States Army, 1914-1997

I walk down our hallway early in the morning,
In the time between the creation of shadows
And the golden brushes of the dawn's first light,
Wondering how to soothe Madame Pamela's grief,
Asking again what to say before the family,
And your picture on the wall confronts me.
There, you gaze at me with the unbridled confidence
Only a young man can feel so sure about,
Out of the camera's stolen moment for eternity,
And on, and on beyond, with the badge of St. Luke
On your breast—you are a medic in the war to clean up
What was left after *The War to End All Wars*.

I remember again the last dwindling days of your life,
When you removed yourself from the family;
You lost interest and you stopped caring about being here.
In the time of dying, you even told me once
You shouldn't have withdrawn from all the rest of us—
But we too know you did, and we watched you leave.
In the final days, with such a frail and sunken little frame,
With such long hair and overflowing beard,
You seemed to tilt at windmills and run blindly,
Insanely pushing us away, off into the distance.

But in the end, unlike the Spaniard's weak delusion,
Your march into the setting sun is no quixotic meander.
Your thin, bony shoulders, arms and legs are wrapped
In a greater strength than what we ever knew.
In the Battle of the Bulge, with your finger
In the dike of the terrible, horrible carnage there,
Your spine took on a different alloy and now
At the end, after all the trouble and the drink,
Your profile's changed.

I see you shadowed on the wall here, your confident stare
Almost challenging, despite the many years and tears.
As the sun puts its fingers down the hall, I become wiser.

> *When we say good-bye today*
> *Among the hills studded with stones,*
> *You go into the sunset's glory*
> *Riding an old, tired horse*
> *And lifting a damaged lance, for sure;*
> *But your shoulders are square,*
> *Your spine is straight*
> *And your journey, triumphal.*

Post-Traumatic Grief Grace

There is a place we go
After many months of struggling
With deep and grinding grief.
The aching loss and the hurt
Of the early days remain, of course,
But the spirit is quieter, softer in this time.
The feelings become almost comfortable,
Like the sides of an old and valued coin,
And rest in a calm and still silence.
They won't ever go away;
They abide behind everything.
But the landscape is surer now,
As strength and certainty return
And the adventures begin again—
Slower and more unfamiliar, maybe,
But they have returned for our journey,
For us to grow again
And to stretch, to flex our love.

After the Summer Fires

It is not a mellow and content sigh, this heavy rain.
Its force is too persistent to be spilling lazily,
As an afterthought to a higher existence, or accidentally,
As a side-effect of grander, more important matters.

No, the heavens will stay to fight in the streets today.
The rain comes express now with the purpose of cleansing
The dirt and disease from the skin of the slum.

But the duckling hunches
While he bathes in the insistent drops.
Unmindful of the rain his gritty plumage holds at bay,
He shakes his head, sneers his scorn
And holds the would-be healers in contempt.

He knows the rain will pass away,
And even the puddles will dry.
Only discarded candy wrappers,
Dead chewing gum and other derelicts
Will stay the course to scab up his more intimate wounds.

The wine jugs are watching,
Pleased and willing to be helpful,
From weed clumps and rock piles;
But they sing with a lethargy
Destined for shattered glass and tattered, faded labels.

The tin cans that now sound plunks
To the rhythm of the rains
Will dry up and rust with the other muffled junk,
Becoming sad ads for cheap beers
And crumpled homes for mice.

All these gentle sighs and nice intentions trickle off
The backside of the duckling
And never change the ugliness.
Though things will be pretty in this tiny season of spring,
The interest always softens, mists and drifts away.

Down in Hollywood

There is art in the morning
When mists rise from the hills to the north.
Almost oriental, mysterious dreams
Of flat hilly lines push up from
The white matte finish of the early morning fogs.
Darker shades of gray, they are simply edges
Marked for observation in the dawning light.
Like the paintings of hills on Chinese room dividers
In the Sunset Boulevard flat of my friend,
There is no dimension, but only image and symbol.
In the empty streets the signs purr and promise
Dreams and fantasies to the whole world,
But they are made of squares and circles
And not cubes and spheres.
The fact that I know these are
Real hills and real streets and real signs
Is the appealing mystery of the dreams.
The sun rises and the outlines of the hills clear.
Cars and trucks move along the roads,
And the clarity of the full-blown day
Washes the dreams away in the certain dullness
Of its bulk, its reality and its work.

The Devil Winds

Look here, old-timer, I'm new in town.
What about these desert winds?

> *The Santanas? Yes.*

Do they usually come about this time?

> *After the bean crops are in, yes, and they go on*
> *Until just before the oranges blossom.*

All this grit in the air, I wonder how you people stand it.
Yesterday, there was no smog
And these dead mountains of yours were visible
And the air was clean and my neighbor said,
"Close your windows."

> *Beautiful, ain't it, just before the winds blow?*

The air makes my Dacron polyester shirt crinkle
And the hair on my legs spark.

> *Yes, but there was no smog.*

But it's not as bad as this grit.
It was in my oatmeal this morning!
If they'd do as much to clear up the grit
As they do with these stupid smog devices I'd be happier.

> *Yes, the smog, it is bad; but we've made that ourselves.*
> *Maybe, we'll make it go away, too.*

Yes, maybe, but we should find out how
to stop these desert winds.

> *Yes, but they are like a disease, like a summer cold.*
> *They never kill people, they only irritate them,*
> *And they only last for three days at a time,*
> *Thank God.*

Thank God.

The Monsoon Season

They drift into the old plazas
As the autumn cools to a glow.
Then pitied souls, they tug on
Handouts, shelter and sympathy
Through the winter of sidelong
Southerly warmth from the sun.

They falter later, in the daze
Of white-hot springtime baking,
And blow away in breezy drips,
The oppressed of the hot rain.
Summers, the streets of Tucson
Don't ever house the homeless.

Bright Daggers of Light

As we sit after dinner on the verandah of the old rancho,
Watching the lights of El Paso
Twinkle in the distant dark,
The desert breezes play lightly
Among the cactus and the brush.
Thunderclouds roil over the Mexican mountains
And spit occasional bright daggers of light
Down to the ground.
Thirty miles of open country
Don't seem like a hill of beans
In the midst of the rumbling
Symphonies that jump over the land.
The old men around me smoke cigars and drink brandy
And regard the scene before us in silence and with respect.
They are the managers of my aircraft electronics projects.
They are used to responsibility and authority.
They know unconsciously
To regard with awe the effort it takes
To organize such a monumentally impressive performance,
To make it all come out so beautifully and so right.

I am their leader, they are my team and we build bombers.
I have neither cigar nor brandy, but coffee and prayers.
I have their respect because I am competent
In the things they understand
And because they have my respect and they know it.
They are not comfortable with my faith,
But they accept it as part of the whole package.
With six you get egg roll, they say, and laugh.
They are practical men and not concerned with dreams
Or infinities or subtle nuances.

Over the twinkling of El Paso,
Through the quiet and abiding desert night,
Bright daggers of light flash again
As missives from the south, from Mexico;
In a bit the announcement of their delivery
Arrives on the verandah
Like the signal shots of unknown artillery,
Powerful whether friend or foe.

Sunrise on the Santa Fe Trail

With colored pens the morning comes
To lift the darkness from the land.
The pinks and golds, the violet hues
That yawn above the stretching sand
Are soft and lovely, gentler far
Than scrabbled desert's daylight face.
In the dawn the promise whispers
Better, quiet interludes of grace
To clear the hard and brittle cold,
The chilling loneliness of night,
From out of aching arms and legs
Before the coming, blinding light,
The burned and parching brilliance
Of the desert's high summer day.

The moment calms the weary travelers,
A quiet pause for healing on the way.
Along the Santa Fe, between the trials
Of cactus, rugged hills and sandy sink,
The colored pens of dawn write messages,
Ephemeral lines in disappearing ink.

Miss Andrea

On the occasion of her wedding to Paulie

The Girl in the World came to stay with us in August.
She was a tiny little thing who smiled
When we wrapped her in a little blanket
And put her in her big brother's arms.
She grew up with dolls and lace and more smiles,
Then moved on to jeans and sweatshirts and more smiles,
Then moved on, and on, and on, and on.
Every new thing has been a gift for her to try.
Singing, dancing and acting onstage
Or entertaining us with her Valley Girl shtick
Or teaching us to cook in little vignettes,
She has embraced it all with the grace
And fearlessness only an old soul knows.
The world has been her playground and
She has been delighted always to be in the world,

To be the Girl in the World.

But now there are sounds around about her,
Music and harmonies that speak to our hearts
And fill them with the sense that something *right* is here.
And there are songs being sung quietly, quietly,
Songs that make our eyes crinkle in smiles
Even as we don't quite hear all the words of them.
She *loves* the Man in the Moon and she's smiling;
He's in love with her and he's smiling, *too*.
Now, every new thing will be a gift for *them* to try,
To embrace with all the grace
And fearlessness only old souls know.

So the songs we almost hear are the songs of the angels
And the harmonies are the music of the spheres.
What else *can* it be

>   *When the Man in the Moon loves the Girl in the World*
>   *And the Girl in the World loves the Man in the Moon?*

The Florida Keys

They are little splashes of sand
Dropped into the turquoise sea
Between the continent and Cuba,
Flat specks for seagulls wed
To frames of ornate pirate tales.
Divers find rusted cannonballs
And the occasional doubloon,
But more often they only coast
In the slowly waving current
And count the time as treasure.

Isolated couples are dropped
On the specks by the fast boats
Of locals making an easy living
Selling temporary franchises.
Left alone, entwined together,
They empty champagne bottles
And pretty, woven picnic baskets.
In tune with water kissing sand,
They make slow, over and over,
Gentle pounding, surging love,
The sunlight laughing with them.

When the World Came Down

Roiling chocolate rivers run to the sea
Where the rain forests died and went,
The giant lines of logs afloat, enchained
And dragged in slavery down the arteries
To market, to market for buying fat pigs.

The delicate dances of the different ones
Who made their homes within the forest
Had produced the colors of the rainbow
Within the shadows and long dark corridors
That kept the outside world at bay, baying
For many, many hundreds of fearful moons.
Brilliant colors on the butterfly wings
Were traced in flowers, fungal growth
And even animals who moved along the ways.

Memories within the rain forest had come
From beyond the very beginnings of history.
The secret paths the tribes had tread
Had carried strange and powerful brews
With magic cures and remedies more right
Than any scientific brilliance in the men
Who'd come with vials and syringes through
The ancient rain forest walls of green.

After many centuries of gentle movement
Back and forth between the touching worlds
Of spirit mother and her suckling earth,
The denizens of the rain forest saw
The earth movers of fat slash-and-burn pigs.

When the trees came down nothing grew,
Nothing at all, not the young birds, not
The insects, the strange mushrooms, not
The animals and their prey, nor even the
Humans who understood—only the new ones
With no spirit, no connection, no living
Memory of how the rain forest instructs,
Protects and nourishes the whole family.

With the death of the world even the soil
Broke apart, yielded its life and left, so now
Roiling chocolate rivers run to the sea.

Crusader Rabbit

Ashes, ashes, ashes—
Why do I still try? I cannot stop them.
They will not listen to the agony in my tears.
They will not let me show them
How we've pillaged our sacred places in easy obeisance
To the night-time prostituted gutter-gods
Of sleazy weakness and resentful irresponsibility.
I would shout some more, if I were rested up,

But I'm already dry.
I will turn on bended knee to my own impotent humanity.
I will let them burn with each other,
With all their scorn, with all their laziness,
With all their fear,
Into little piles of aching, regretful loneliness.
Then I will gaze ever afterward into my soul and cry—
Ashes, ashes, ashes.

The Capstone

In the mostly quiet telling of moments,
Beyond the ceremonies and the blessings,
When lengthy meditation has blocked out
The earthiness of the material world,
When I grow bored with remembering truths
Of the most exquisite spiritual nature,
I hear the lilting music of the spheres
And then I know—insanely, I just know—
Why I am here and there and everywhere.

Never Mind, Gautama

He lay in a room with the darkness soothed by sound
And a bottle for his ashtray; staring through the glass,
He sobbed silver tears for the drops upon the grass.
The moon was bright and lonely, falling everywhere;
Dripping through the trees came a silence, long and shrill.
But the ones who'd slept before were sleeping still.

Within the year he lay without and smiled
A life of inner waterfalls; he was himself, drinking deep,
Passing pleasantries and resting on the lawn, asleep.
The sun rose slowly as his ministry came due;
His own awareness bid him pay the coming bill.
But the ones who'd slept before were sleeping still.

Castles in the Sand

I watched celestial temples
    So grand, towering and bright,
Glowing with a deafening song
    And rent by poems of light.

I watched the land below
    Grow green from the rain's fertile caress
And anchor glorious rainbows
    To proclaim the storm's success.

I watched the sea in storm-fury,
    A blue-gray god—raw power
Unaware of the pains we take
    To build our Babel's tower.

And I cringe when I hear you
    Praising the mighty works of man.
We blow bubbles in the wind
    And fashion castles in the sand.

High Mass

A waltz, a lovely waltz,
        begins the easy, graceful trial
Of lofty, fancied pleasantries—
        the usher's finely painted smile.
Empty decadence, a rotting fugue
        that leads the faithful home,
Eats and drinks, lazily devours—
        growing so, and only lately sown.
The groups of wet cantatas,
        dripping, dancing off the walls,
Drill into the sacred wood—
        the hallowed, hollow, dirty halls.
Even now the offerings,
        concertos singing to the sun,
Do nothing for the soul—
        whose trial has just begun.

The Mud Pie Party (A Painting)

It's chocolate rain
In the bright red sky,
Pineapples purple
And posturing high,
Lemon-filled raisins
Waiting for the beat
Of green tomatoes
That fry in the heat.
An open fire roast
By the deep brown sea
Cooks polka-dot limes
For afternoon tea.

Merlin's Passing

As the wizard's health failed,
The nobles in strange costumes
Came from across the mountains
And over the wind-blown seas.

They didn't come to leave gifts,
But only to have the old man
In their lives one more time.
His great-grandchildren watched,

Not completely understanding
The power of their Opah-Opah,
Not feeling in their family
The exquisite honor of his life,

Not seeing the bonds of respect
That pulled so many comrades
So many leagues to his side,
To be a gentle comfort to him

In the last days of his life.
Finally, it wasn't his honor,
But his body that failed,
And the legions who loved him

Celebrated his last triumph
With great and joyful sounds,
Even as they cried in their loss
With silent, discretionary tears.

Yorba Linda Celebration

We got these four presidential-type fellas
Coming into town from all over the country
To make a big to-do about this here library with the roses
And the funny architecture.
Now, don't get me wrong; I'm a citizen and a patriot.
And I expect they's all, all honorable men.
Hell, how can ya become president
If ya ain't an honorable man?
'Course they's honorable men;
They reached the top of the heap.
Ya know what heap I mean. 'Course ya do.

Politics.

We flush our dollars off to them, all for good causes,
And so little trickles back it seems like an accident,
Like there's a leak in the tank somewhere
They don't know about.
Then we all scream and holler for more.
Anyway, they's guaranteed
The best practitioners of the craft.
Every one of these fellas made it to the top, by gum,
Like cream floating up over fresh, sweet milk.

Well, we gonna honor these four presidential-type fellas
By treating 'em like they put their pants on
Both legs at once.
We gonna listen to their speeches all day long
Just like they had something important to say.
We even gonna allow our little politicians
Some money for plaques
To commemorate what a grand and glorious day of honor
We had here for these four presidential-type fellas.

Now, don't get me wrong; I'm a citizen and a patriot.
I'm as pleased as the next one
About Yorba Linda's day in the sun.
I ain't here to bury these fellas, just here to praise 'em.
Hell, they's the ones for decades
Been running our government to where
It is now, so big and important and complicated.
Hell, it has so many good things for every single one of us
We can't even keep track of 'em all,
Let alone pick and choose the ones we need.

> *Hell, it's so wonderful I reckon*
> *We'll never thank 'em enough,*
> *Even though we're pitching*
> *These four presidential-type fellas*
> *More home-town honor than*
> *I expect we've spewed out for a long time.*
> *And I already said,*
> *They's all, all honorable men.*
> *'Course, now, ya understand,*
> *Dried-out cow pies float, too.*

Buddha on the Mountain

I watch from Within,
And from Without;
I live, therefore I love.

My love, my love, my most grievous love.

I know the puddle-self,
The depths below,
And the heights above.

My love, my love, my most grievous love.

The View from Murchison Park

In the gathering twilight *El Paso* and *Ciudad Juarez*
lie together by the river,
But they stay at arm's length
    across the bridges during the winter chill.
Though the days may be warm and gentle in the sun,
    the nights are icy cold.
Lights come on in *El Paso*
    and fires start to flicker in *Ciudad Juarez*.
Smoke begins in delicate pillars rising
    from shacks of adobe and wood,
Thickens and spreads over neighborhoods
    with few lights and many fires,
Then ambles through the dusk and the night,
    along the prevailing breezes
And past the blue Mexican lights,
    over the river to the wealthy yellow ones
Of the neighborhoods draped
    around the Franklyns and poured out easterly,
Clean neighborhoods with electricity
    and warm with natural gas furnaces.
Much is said of the evening smells,
    the pollution, the winter smog problem,
Of the environmental disaster
    with which the government *refuses* to deal,
And of the dirty Mexican criminals
    carelessly burning wood, and *stuff*.
The lights of *El Paso* go out at night
    when the furnaces are turned down,
But the fires of *Ciudad Juarez* flicker and dance
    all through the chilling dark.

So, there is conflict each year
>   between the two old cities in the Pass.
The argument caused by the winter smog
>   only lasts the season, however.
When it is warm, the Mexican ecological bandits
>   light only cooking fires.

White Lace at Low Tide

Wispy lines of blue-green waves
Break gently side to side along the
>   wide and level sandy strand,
Urging fingers of flat water,
>   insistent puddles, onto the beach.
White embroidered foam left over
>   from the slow roll of each wave
Covers the flat expanse of sand
Like delicate dreams stretching
>   over the dingy drudgery of life.
Beautiful tapestries spread out
>   for the short times of the flow.
When the water runs back to the sea,
>   the foam sinks and settles,
Leaving with the breaker's ebb.
Here and there on the deserted beach,
Traces of the froth remain
To mark their forms upon the sand,
>   like ambitions tatted so long
That lives change, and mold themselves
>   into realized dreams.

Cigarette Spirits

Silently spinning, spiraling wisps,
Wandering from this cancer stick—
Oh yearning habit, mine—
Do you wander where you please?
Do you know the freedom and the joy,
Which you claim you really have?
Do you heed the poet's words
By his snowy woods, so dark?
I tend to doubt you,
Free-lance pilgrims, spilling outward,
Searching for your souls.
Slow your pace to mine
And talk a bit of jokes.
Watch, perhaps, a flower

    Or two.

Then go again to Gothic places,
Silvered with your gutter-robes.
There, the Guides you'll have
You'll never know; those,
The Guest you haven't noticed yet.
The wall is paper-thin, but I hint now
Lest you run into a post.
Watch the greens and golds,
And, too, the ever-present grays
Beneath your smoky stair.
I'll meet you at the end—
I've been there, too, you know.
Do you wander, do you,
Silently spinning, spiraling wisps?

Hope

Seven times the candle sighed
    To tell them she still lived,
        Though they were certain she had died.

Seven times she cried aloud
    To lure them from the streets,
        But they were happy with the crowd.

Seven times she sang a hymn
    To ease the scorn and hate
        That ate them up from deep within.

Seven times she screamed and sobbed
    Distress to those who sighed,
        And sighing, shrugged and blindly robbed.

Seven times she deftly stole
    The selfish love they'd labeled
        Good and gilded 'round with gold.

Seven times she sank
    Into the mires of discontent
        To heal the blind, the longing and the rank.

And seven times she suckled seeds
    That still remained to sprout,
        Kissing softly the Hand that feeds.

Morning's Eyes

                Ah,
                Sweep
                The air
                                  Through
                Morning's eyes,
Touch
                The dawn
                                  With prayer.
                Listen
While the
                Song birds
                                  Offer praise
                And thanks
In crystal
                Dew-drop
                                  Symphonies.
                Taste
The newness
                In
                The air,
                Ah.

Navajo Respite

When the rain comes in the afternoon
The old People stick their tongues out
To taste the pure, cool water
Father pours from the skies.

The skin around their eyes
Crinkles in silent, knowing smiles;
Just now, the dust and heat of the mesas
Are pushed back down into the land
With watery and then muddy massages.

There is a small time of quiet enjoyment
Out among the drops, where everyone knows
The hardness of the summer won't return
Until after Father sends his rainbow
To touch the red rocks and cathedral canyons
Of the land He gave the People.

Apology for Winter

It is said there is no winter in Los Angeles,
But what is said is wrong.
In the winter even the rocks hunker down
And wait for the coming of spring.
Although without clouds, the days are still gray.
There is only mild warmth in the distant sun.
White mists come out of the mouths
Of the hikers who enjoy the close-in canyons
Round about the basin filled with noise.
The hills become dry and jagged and brown.

Rustling the dead and broken grasses,
The field mice gather grain
And only fear the hawks that fly above.
The cold-blooded snakes lie dormant,
Drugged with the winter's call to sleep
And hidden under rocks and in their holes.
In the spaces between the small noises there is quiet
And it is acknowledged by the hikers
With the nods and smiles of those
Who know and share the secret understanding
Of the time of waiting in the hills.

There are cold waters in the streams
And they move slowly, dropping over rocks
With almost melancholy murmurs in their passing.
Only after the warm rains will the hills
Soften with a mantle of new green whiskers
And the creeks swell with the pride of living high.
They settle in now and wait for the coming of spring,
For the warm sun and damp earth and brilliant green,
For new little bodies scampering about
To learn the paths of safety and the places of danger.

The brassy cheeping of young birds
Impatient for the size and weight of flight
Will come again, as well, in the spring,
But instead there is silent patience in the winter,
And even the rocks hunker down.

Sierra Valley Shower

The orange mists to the sides of the dying sun
    loosed silver light in slanting rays of royalty.
The billowing thickness of reborn Byzantine heavens
    gilded its girth with gold.
The sultry, sifting air turned soft
    in expectation of the sunset's gaudy show.
Gray shades muffled the lilting song of spring-grown green
    on the leaves of the trees.
In the distant haze a deer lifted his nobility
    and froze in a salute, a magic and majestic trance.
The babbling denizens of the forest's deeper memories
    waited in nervous quietude.
Between the trees a creek gurgled childish enthusiasms
    into the settling stillness.
The mantle of the receding light dripped
    hushing revelations of almost lost involvement.
The preparation was complete, the orchestra still,
    just waiting for the Master of the Dance.
The mountains stretched and settled in their shadows
    for the dawn of the coming night.
With subtle streaks and murmuring patters
    the quiet fled and the twilight wandered in.

Power

There is one, or must be one,
Hailed they say
From the depths of the soul's need
In a universe of randomness
And inscrutable stochastic processes.
Somehow, life has sprung impossibly
Out of the ancient mineral kingdom.
But there is a star that was no star,
Which stepped out of the black firmament
And moved according to the Law of Laws
In circles turning within circles,
So that scholars in succeeding millennia
Should ask questions studiously
Among the wise men of each age
About it's going before truly wise men
Who stepped out of their cozy dens
And stood under the Star in Bethlehem.
All of them sneer at what they call fables,
But each one of them assumes
From the depths of the ego's regard
Inscrutable stochastic processes;
Indeed, each one sees a universe of randomness
Where there is none.

Perspective

One man's trash glistens
In the silvery moonlight;
He found no treasure.

The Tucson Table

After Sunday breakfast in the big house on the mesa,
Sipping coffee on the verandah in his old iron chair,
The ranch's master squints wrinkled eyes in the sun.
He rubs the turquoise and silver buckle on his belt,
Extends his long, still-strong arms up into the air.
He yawns, stretches his legs, eyes his leather boots,
Breathing deeply, slowly, scanning the ambling lands.
In the distant haze, down to the south over Mexico,
Billowing cloud towers signal trouble for later on,
Strong winds and maybe driving rains before sundown.
The concerns, though, are for his sons and not him;
For him it is morning in the spring, a warming time
With new green grasses bending in the aimless breeze.
The deep blue sky pushes soft sunshine into his face,
Caressing old eyes that are closed not to shut out,
But to remember the easy rests and quiet nourishings
Where he paused between hard times and heavy burdens,
Taking on water for the wellspring of his character.

A Still, Small Wind

Any summer day
The world of our efforts
Can swirl in a breezy atmosphere of things accomplished
And things left for the future.
A soft, creeping mood begins with a haze
On the slopes ahead of us
And trickles down—digesting the attentive quiet
And diligent music of the norms.

Any summer day

She is here when we feel her—
In her embrace our wills and our industry don't exist.
Drifting 'round in an unforgettably non-existent eddy,
She soothes the burns of our ambitions.
Strange thoughts and lazy contemplations
And memories of nothing that remain memories
Haunt the air and the trees.

Any summer day

Can bring an afternoon of happy friends and soft talk
And no work—and then she knows us well.
In those hours we're hoisted from
The endless ring that is our world.
Then we smile at inward sighs
And laugh through souls and sacred cows,
Smoking cigarettes with a strange taste
That really hasn't changed.

Any summer day

The grass can weave its fingers
Through our yielding bones
To free them of a crystalline cold.
Careful not to step where cement ends and lawn begins,
The provosts fear our madness ever there.
They're wrong, but I wish they weren't.
She leaves with the night,
But she's been there—and will be on

Any summer day

The Three Musketeers

The laughs, on all sides of our holy fraternities,
Guide us with unerring ease to the thinly disguised
Inanities of which mankind takes wholehearted part.

The glances, quickly swallowed and taken back when
Once they're discovered, show no hatred, but rather
Bellicose loneliness, sad, regretting, but cowardly.

Words—always the words—of aggressive warning
Offer no friendly greeting, but twist in and out of
The souls of both sides, asking perversely for love.

Valedictory for Megan

*Major Megan Malia Leilani McClung,
United States Marine Corps, 1972-2006*

Well, young lady,
We never expected to be here,
Saying good-bye to you this way.

We imagine you wrapped in the arms of God,
Beaming and smiling, but even now
Squirming and ready to jump down,
To run around and explore the Court.
We see you grin at God and touch His face;
But finally you leap from His lap,
Getting into things one after another,
Your red hair giving them glimpses of your brightness
As you sprint around the Kingdom.
The angels are only a little scandalized,
Because they delight in you as much as we have.
We are so proud of you
And all you've accomplished
That our hearts touch momentarily
The family of man and the face of God.

Well, Marine,
We never expected to be here,
Saying good-bye to you this way
In Arlington's December,
The caisson coming over the hill
To the slow beat of the drum
And the red and blue of your comrades
In stark contrast to the gray all over;
But your faithfulness and ours require it.

And so, we've gathered here to tell you
That we love you and we appreciate you.
You know our affection for you
Abides in the stories we tell.

> *And you know through our tears,*
> *Marine, we salute you.*

The Leader

Just about midstream he struggles valiantly,
Fighting against the current and overcoming,
Moving slowly and stroke by stroke upstream
To the little beach he glimpses off ahead.

At the softer sides of the river's reach,
And out of the manly challenge in midstream,
His fellows move along behind him a little,
Not often very much in sight of the beach,
But trusting him and sure, swimming easily.
They arrive, too, at the place he has chosen,
But they arrive without any heavy breathing.

Not so depleted and so needing gentle rest,
They appreciate and enjoy the little beach
Even more than he does in his exhaustion.
Eyes closed, he feels his satisfaction deep.
Their lives are the better for his leadership
And they offer him the best of all they have.

He's pleased, but really has no interest now.
His journey wouldn't *be* without their company,
But his life is in *it* and not where it goes.

The Mountain Corral

The pen had its weak points,
The mares didn't know where,
But the stallion tested them
And knew it didn't matter.

They were fed and they were safe.
The mountain pines were tall
And stretched their shade over the pen,
So it was comfortable and easy.

There were weak points in the pen,
But it still didn't matter,
Until the fire ate the trees.

The stallion pushed on the points
Only he knew would give 'way,
And so finally it did matter.

He broke open the mountain pen
And led his brood to safety.

Solitary Moon Night Sky

Ah,
          Sniff
          The silence
          Of a soft,
Solitary
                    Moon
Night sky.
                    Silver clouds
          Dabble
          Sheep's wool
          Bits
                    Of shadows
Here
                  And there.
Senses
          Sifting
          The knowledge
          Softly sigh
Ah.

Laguna in the Winter

For now, it is winter in Laguna.
The sea and the sun are there, but not so many people.
To the northwest in the shoals,
      is the old white-covered rock,
Which remains the home of pelicans and gulls.
The dark blues and greens of the sea spread and ripple
In their shades out, and out and out
      to the island of Catalina.
Toward the southeast in the morning sun
There are silver sparkles dancing on the sea.
In close along the beach, there is a white foamy lace
In the water left after the breakers pound against the sand.
They do their work over and over and over again
To pull by bits and pieces into the ocean's deeper dales,
But the sand holds firm and stays the season.
In an ages-old agreement,
      the tides put back whatever leaves,
And Laguna does not slip below the waves.
The gulls hold their councils on the sand,
      turning their heads
Into the chilling wind that whips off the winter waves.
Local families bring their children here
And the little ones walk in the sand and point at the birds
And collect bits and pieces of shells for their rooms.
Their garb, even in the bright sunshine,
Is long pants and heavy coats and scarves.
The winter sun is bright, but the wind is crisp.
It burns the cheeks and waters the eyes
Of those who wander slowly
      along the wooden promenade.
Without the tourists of the summer
      and the food they bring,
The birds that gather along the ocean coast
Rediscover their integrity and move again with the grace
Of those to whom it is given to soar on the wind.

The people of Laguna regain the sand and the sea
    in the off-season.
There will come again the warm winds
    and throngs of summer,
And tourists in tiny bathing suits will crowd out the birds,
Except for the ones that stoop to begging and thieving.

    But for now, it is winter in Laguna.

Evensong for Helena

The moon shines its silver through the clear night sky,
A beacon shedding light to the upturned eye.
In Madame Modjeska's home, sycamores smile
And the oaks restrain their rustling for a while.
Rosemary and sage infuse the dry night air
And rabbits hop the trails, careful and aware.
The still of the night and the phase of the moon
Draw the canyon's dwellers out to hear the tune
The gang of Juan Flores sang about the hole
Where all their treasures disappeared, all the gold
That no hunter in the decades since has found.
Neighbor smiles at neighbor; no one makes a sound.

San Francisco's Intermission

Treading softly, the melting golden orb
Oozes fog's feet under the burning bridge
And into the slow lapping of the inner bay.

The harsh, croaking sounds of kindled minds
Die in the silence beneath the misty gray hush—
Echoes of mysteries forgotten for the night.

The muffled mantle of its creeping indifference
Makes quiet the kindling of the recent past
And buries the gold in an opulent obscurity.

Day's End

Noisy minds settle,
Melting golden orb reclines,
Glows rose and beams peace

Mesa Verde

Spruce Tree House rises in a half-cavern,
Carved from the mesa's side and left open.
In glorious ranks, watching the setting sun,
What was a community of pale brown colors,
An adobe and stone town in the light of day,
Is burnished gold, then deeper copper reds,
Then melts into spreading nests of shadows
As night ascends from the canyon bottoms,
Following dusk up the sides of the cliffs,
Over the careful blocks of deserted homes,
Beyond the highest crown of the half-cavern
To the brush and stumpy trees atop the mesa.

Later in the still coolness of the evening,
Under the broad silver brush of the moon,
There is a holiness mixed into the mystery
Of the old dwellings, of Spruce Tree House,
And I from my vantage point across the way,
Lift up a thankful heart before the sight
Left behind, the sacred dreams of a people
Who offered it then to God as a sacrifice,
Giving it to other men in centuries to come
With all its questions, its gentle serenity.
Even the birds are hushed, and I am pleased,
Pleased to worship in the ancient sanctuary.

Mister Matt

In the garden outside after the early morning rains
There is dew glistening on the long blades of grass
Across the lawn and over at the edge of the patio.

In one spot, just where the sunlight splashes in,
The delicate lace and winding form of a spider's web
Present jeweled strands of glory with watery pearls.

In this quiet interlude before the day begins
I am at peace and full of love
For the world my God has given me.

And I am overwhelmed.

I mumble thanks, incoherent prayers under my breath
And rising in the mists of steaming coffee from my mug.
I am content and there is nothing more to add.

But then my toddling son comes out to join the scene,
Not seeing me at the kitchen window,
He steps resolutely from the other end of the patio.

What I have accepted as my gift he perceives as his,
Giggles his own appreciation as I have smiled mine.
He teeters to the illumined web and plops down close.

I think in panic of sweeping him up in my arms
To keep him from hurting himself or getting wet—
But really to distract him and save the beauty.

Before I can move, he reaches out a tiny finger, points,
And carefully pokes the center of the spider's creation
Without rending the silken lines or shattering the jewels.

Watching the sun's rays through its wiggling form,
He laughs, turns away from the web
And contemplates a drop of dew upon the grass.

He puts his face down very close and slowly, oh so slowly,
Puts his tongue out to touch the glistening globe.
When the drop finally collapses onto the tip of his tongue
He squeals with delight, claps his hands again, sits quietly.

> *Gratitude floods in on me; I left him free.*
> *What was fullness for me once is now increased.*
> *My son, in his own way, loves even what I love*
> *And is learning to pray in a language I recognize.*

Grand Canyon Treasure

The Havasupai dreams come drifting, falling,
Filtering down through the certain rocks
And on out of the older right side
To make peace with the competition
Of fixed patterns and sinister categories.
At the bottom, in a splash of sun,
Light blue-green washes over low pedestals
And bright trees hang in the still air
To frame what is magnificent tranquility,
Not above the world and overlooking it,
Unaffected and bemused by the storms,
But down and down within the world,
Feeling the activity and the concern,
Yet content in the centered peace
Of what lies, after all, between and beneath.

Winging West

The caverns between the cloud towers
Pull me into them with siren shadows.
Playing, I bounce around in my mind,
Off the white edges of broken pillows
And always further on and on, sliding
Down into the darker spaces below,
Where black pine forests stretch out,
Then shadowy hints of farms flow by,
Then craggy landscapes of desolation
And many miles of empty, open ranges,
Then a few lonely, wandering rivers,
And finally houses and streets and lights.

I might be living among the shadows,
But I dream between the cloud towers.

Deus ex Machina

The eagle soars across the bright spring sky,
His feathers barely ruffling in the air;
Out of their sight, he rides the wind up high,
And his eyes see movement everywhere.

Enmeshed below in worries all their own,
The little creatures thus contend and try
To settle troubles only they have sown;
Then he dives—moves at last and leaves the sky.

Since his only sound is the wind above,
The warning's just a shadow o'er their fight.
Changing little lives, he leaves on the ground
Bewildered shock and not Minerva's light.

The Whistling Wind and the Crashing Sea

The Bread of Life stands above us, waiting quietly now,
Letting us feel His gentle presence in the short silences,
His love for us whispering between our screams.
We push away from Him, push back and rush headlong
Into terrible battles we ourselves have created to fight,
To stand proudly as the victors, feet on the vanquished,
Or to lie abjectly, crushed in our submission and defeat.
When we've spun the webs, played each part to the end,
When the competition carries neither thrill nor agony,
Only in the sunset of reflections and exhausted ambitions
Do we see the truth enough to turn aside, inside ourselves.
With open arms and overflowing hearts, *finally* we affirm
Our right to *have* the Bread of Life, to drink of His cup,
To feel the peace and overwhelming joy of what it means
To inherit earth, the whistling wind and the crashing sea.

Noble

Old Noble spent most of his time
Alone except for the dog.
He tended the western oil lease
And cared for the worn old wells.
He kept things running when he could
And let the young foreman know
When there were things to fix.
The dog traveled with him
On the seat beside the lunch pail.
It was just a seedy little mutt,
But Noble had a soft heart for it,
Took care like it was his horse,
And like he'd die without it there.
They stayed together on the lease,
Riding herd on broken old wells
And rusting pipes in weedy places
For the better part of a dozen years.
Then one of the young men
Found old Noble stone cold dead,
Slumped over the wheel of his truck.
They tried to feed the dog,
But it wouldn't eat at all.
It just slowed down, slowed down
And died in a month or so,
And followed its master off
To wherever old cowboys go.

Semi-Precious and Incomplete

I walked amid the sifting sands,
Whistling softly to the wind wailing
   and to the surf pounding.
The sun-gold cliffs I'd stumbled down
Stood silent witness to my quest
   for the dim-crowned queen.
The gray birds fled before me,
   so I thought they'd lost my call.
But the gulls, wheeling,
   cried their song in answer,
Calling senate 'round my feet.
They, now in circle—and I, forgotten—
Watched a wave, a long, unbroken line,
Peaking translucent blue
   along the placid green and white.
Pealing off, it slid to the left,
   turning without any pain or sound
Again to green and white—
   following the lone black gull.
She flew into the sun and blinded me.
When again I had my sight I was alone
And bore the brunt of one great wave.
The showering, shimmering beads fell in
   upon themselves and me;
They rose again as silver mist.
I watched, and through the independent wisps
I found that you were gone.

Perspiring Perspective

    Piqued are those people there who did and do
    Count angels on pinheads
          And kill Abel
                And envy Richard Corey
                      And stone the Pacific
                And curse the moody clouds
        And say of it all, *Reality.*
    Their fire licks the black of its
    Pictured frame.

Circles Within Circles

The spinning, grinning spirits of the Hall
Swirl in psychedelic mud and alcoholic hues,
Twisting their hosts into grotesque shades
Of bygone dreams and vacant, empty memories.
Their ghosts are lost and their wisdom dies
In lingering draughts from foggy mugs of brine.
The chamber oozes in and out of the tinny sounds
And rusted gutter-mists of fortune's lucky few.

Its future slowly dying, the giant Hall is choked
With wasted thistles bearing viper's love
And brittle shells of mica from the kings.
Compassionate relatives have made the clock run slow,
But their concern doesn't help—
The innocent irresponsible are milling, glancing fervently.
The sign on the door reads: No Exit.

Always Aloft

Honor floats on the wind
Like a silent hawk,
Then screeches at moves
It doesn't ever like
And strikes furiously
With righteous talons,
Ripping and tearing
Pieces of complacency
And chunks of compromise
Limb from bony limb.

Sinewy knowledge is left
For us to chew and chew,
To feel the places where
What wasn't in our plans
Has made them worthless;
And bloody guilt drips
Over our minds and hands,
Who learned and forgot
That like a silent hawk,
Honor floats on the wind.

The Fruit of the Tree

When the law is used
To rob Peter to pay Paul,
Tyranny blossoms

Peace in Our Time

The players gathered by the sound
And sought to put things where
They ought by right to be.
Perhaps the Lady missed them all,
And spilled her burning gold
From the pebbles of their chances.
Perhaps the air that filtered
Through their eyes and beat
Against their walls had grown
    Stale.

I'm buried there and cannot tell.
The rain is dark and soothing
To my soul and what burned then.
My hand is emptied of the sand
That began my quest for peace—
The import of another time.
My lack of gold I hold secure,
And what I've forgotten for now,
I'll remember maybe tomorrow.

Karmic Strings

The moon drips eerie, wistful loneliness
On shadows in my mind.
Somewhere, very softly, I hear the weary,
Aching sobs of those I once knew well.
My fingers cannot touch their lips to stop the guilt I feel,
For that somewhere—very softly now—that somewhere is
Far too distant in my past.

The Mystery of the Pipes

The lines of kilted warriors are silent, smiling easily,
When all at once they put their lips to blowpipes
And the drummers rattle snares and boom a beat.
The lines of pipers move into the darkened stadium,
Move the white-hot spotlights with them, too,
And fill the air with the royal, haunting sounds
Of acts and battles full of heroes, glories grandiose.
Across the seas and back through many centuries
The bagpipes always sent their eerie martial music
On ahead to cut and chill the spines of enemies,
To fill the friendly breasts of allies with broad hope—
And, of course, to swell and swagger lines of Scots.
Now, the soldiers play and dance and serve the kingdom
With their grace and easy skill before approving crowds.

But in the shadows up behind the pipes and drums
I see the ghostly forms of others in the shades
That swirl as fog around the feet of thousands
As they stand to fight across the moors and peat,
To stop the bitter enemies, the English foreigners.
The battle is most perilous, and even lost before begun,
But the calling of the pipes comes cutting through,
Rolling over lines and lines and lines of kilts,
And tens of thousands all move out and down the hills
With fearful pride and prayers—and all for naught.

The slaughter hides around the edges of the pipes,
And terrible, infinite sadness lurks in the shadows
Beyond the swelling pride their sounds induce in me.
I am a part of the awful scene, so foreign now
And nowhere even hinted at in how I love the pipes.
Though here I swell with pleasure and with pride,
I never heed their sounds today without remembering
The waiting long ago, then the stepping out to death.

Autumn Leaves

The box in the corner,
Coughing up sounds for quarters and the like,
Asks me why I wait.
Throbbing through my skull
And dancing on the vibrant air of sacred spaces,
It shakes loose some memories of the present.
Kissing the flowering walls, it withers them red.

You fool! Why watch for faces that have died
To drift through the open door?
They've gone away; they know nothing of the past,
Nor of a second birth for Technicolor times!
They've gone!
They left with your summer days,
And what you have is now!

Canary

Glorious songster,
Bursting yellow tuxedo,
Little bird singing.

Sparkles of Golden Sunshine

She lights in my mind during the quiet times,
And comes forward to play with my concentration.
For others she is a gifted actress and a lovely singer
And for me she also is these things,
But there is more.
Through the tunnels of time I hold her close to me
And walk with her over ancient stones
And say the words of our wedding before an altar
That sent missionaries into sixth-century Scotland.
I race with her down the road to a doctor
Who saves her life
And she stays with me a little longer.
I watch her as she's watching the children play,
With the sun catching her hair
And lighting the tips of her lashes
And there is golden warmth flowing out from her
To lift up everything in my world.
Her smile brings me peace;
Gentle, bouncing harmony invades the air
All around me.
And when she turns to me and laughs,
I am thrown giggling up into the clouds
To breathe the wispy cotton
And fetch her cooing doves down from there.
She carries with her every day
The gift of a brightly colored *amen* to my life.
Every day I watch her when she's not aware
And I drink a potion of her gift.
It is so little an amount she doesn't even know,
But it is so much my whole world dances in
Sparkles of golden sunshine

.

Alphabetical Poem List – Dates and Pages

A Still, Small Wind	1966	68
After the Summer Fires	1966	42
Always Aloft	1991	85
Anno Domini MCMLXXIX	1990	13
Apology for Winter	1992	64
Autumn Leaves	1968	88
Between Sinner and Saint	1991	16
Between Weed and Grain	1990	24
Bright Daggers of Light	1989	46
Buddha on the Mountain	1967	57
Canary	2016	88
Castles in the Sand	1964	53
Cigarette Spirits	1967	60
Circles Within Circles	1966	84
Crusader Rabbit	1965	51
Curves and Lines	1990	14
Day's End	2016	76
Deus ex Machina	1990	80
Down in Hollywood	1990	43
Easy Does It	1990	15
Evensong for Helena	1988	75
Every Day in Every Way	1968	28
Fog's Night Mysteries	1990	21
For Bud	1997	40
Gentle Caress	1987	11
Grand Canyon Treasure	1990	79
High Mass	1971	54
Hope	1968	61
How Precious Her Happiness	1988	22
Hurless Barton Park	1990	20
I Pray You, Comrade Chairman, Go Gently	1987	35
In the Dalliance before the Dawn	1990	27
Interlude	1992	30
It Is Good	1972	36

Just for the Record	1973	31
Karmic Strings	1966	86
Laguna in the Winter	1986	74
Living Through It All	1993	25
Marriage	1984	21
Merlin's Passing	1990	55
Mesa Verde	1985	77
Miss Andrea	2016	48
Mister Matt	1987	78
Morning's Eyes	1969	62
My Grandfather's People	1986	17
Navajo Respite	1986	63
Never Mind, Gautama	1967	52
Noble	1983	82
Not Free Enough to Try	1990	23
Old Times, End Times, New Times	1990	18
On Tour	1991	37
Peace in Our Time	1967	86
Perspective	2016	66
Perspiring Perspective	1965	84
Post-Traumatic Grief Grace	2013	41
Power	1990	66
San Francisco's Intermission	1968	76
Santa Claus	2016	13
Semi-Precious and Incomplete	1966	83
Sierra Valley Shower	1990	65
Solitary Moon Night Sky	1969	73
South of Mendocino	1970	31
Sparkles of Golden Sunshine	1988	89
Sunrise on the Santa Fe Trail	1989	47
The American Dream	1978	38
The Butterfly	1967	34
The Capstone	1982	52
The Devil Winds	1973	44
The Eyes of God	1971	29
The Florida Keys	1989	49

The Fountain of Youth	1988	32
The Fruit of the Tree	2016	85
The High Road	1966	26
The Leader	1993	71
The Melody that Never Was	1995	33
The Monsoon Season	1990	45
The Mountain Corral	1990	72
The Mud Pie Party (A Painting)	1992	54
The Mystery of the Pipes	1988	87
The Three Musketeers	1965	69
The Tucson Table	1987	67
The View from Murchison Park	1988	58
The Water Gate	1986	15
The Whistling Wind and the Crashing Sea	1994	81
Valedictory for Megan	2006	70
Wanderlust	1997	23
When the World Came Down	1992	50
White Lace at Low Tide	1997	59
White Mountain	1997	12
Winging West	1997	80
With Apologies to Paul	1988	39
Yorba Linda Celebration	1994	56
Yorba Linda Sabbath	1987	26

About the Author

John Forrest Harrell grew up in Huntington Beach, California, in the 1950s and early 1960s. Now known as Surf City, it was then a little oil town along a beach with surf that was perfect for body-surfing—and so there was *always* something to do. He began writing poetry in high school and published his first poem as a sophomore at Harvey Mudd College in Claremont, California. Graduating with a B. S. in mathematics, he also completed an informal degree in 20th century American literature (coordinated for him by his HMC literature professors) at Pomona College. He has served in a variety of capacities on the Executive Board of the California State Poetry Society and the Editorial Board of the *California Quarterly* since the late 1980s.

A retired engineering executive, program manager and satellite data systems scientist, Dr. Harrell holds advanced degrees in management, economics, management information systems, information systems and technology, sacred theology, and theology. Besides continuing as an information scientist, he is an Austrian School economist and a Celtic Catholic theologian. As his children and grandchildren are known to opine, Grandpa *still* doesn't know what he wants to be when he grows up, but—and he points it out often—only growing old is mandatory.

www.ingramcontent.com/pod-product-compliance
Lightning Source LLC
Chambersburg PA
CBHW032031230426
43671CB00005B/275